DIY Guide: Repairing PAR Lights, 12V SMPS, 5V SMPS, and Pixel LED

Raja Sekhar

Published by Raja Sekhar, 2023.

DIY GUIDE: REPAIRING PAR LIGHTS, 12V SMPS, 5V SMPS, AND PIXEL LED

First edition. August 10, 2023.

ISBN: 979-8223170976

Written by Raja Sekhar.

ABOUT THE AUTHOR

RajaSekhar is a seasoned professional in the field of lighting and electronics repairs. With over 10 years of experience in the lighting industry, RajaSekhar has gained extensive knowledge and expertise in repairing PAR Lights, 12V SMPS, 5V SMPS, and Pixel LED systems.

From a young age, RajaSekhar developed a passion for tinkering with electronics and exploring the inner workings of various devices. His curiosity and dedication led him to pursue a career in technical repairs, specialising in lighting fixtures and power supplies. Over the years, RajaSekhar has worked with event organisers, earning a reputation for his exceptional troubleshooting skills and ability to bring malfunctioning equipment back to life.

RajaSekhar firmly believes in the power of sharing knowledge and empowering others to take control of their repairs. Recognizing the lack of accessible resources for DIY enthusiasts and aspiring technicians in the lighting industry, RajaSekhar decided to write the DIY Guide: Repairing PAR Lights, 12V SMPS, 5V SMPS, and Pixel LED. His goal is to provide a comprehensive resource that simplifies complex repair processes, equipping readers with the confidence and skills needed to tackle common issues in these essential lighting components.

Through this guide, RajaSekhar shares not only his technical expertise but also his passion for empowering individuals to understand and repair their lighting equipment. He believes that everyone has the potential to become a capable troubleshooter and hopes that this book will inspire readers to explore the fascinating world of lighting repairs.

RajaSekhar's DIY Guide: Repairing PAR Lights, 12V SMPS, 5V SMPS, and Pixel LED is a testament to his commitment to excellence and his dedication to helping others navigate the intricacies of lighting repairs. With his guidance, readers can confidently embark on their own repair journeys, ensuring the longevity and optimal performance of their lighting systems.

INTRODUCTION

Welcome to the DIY Guide: Repairing PAR Lights, 12V SMPS, 5V SMPS, and Pixel LED. This comprehensive eBook aims to provide you with step-by-step instructions and troubleshooting techniques to help you repair and maintain these essential lighting components. Whether you're an aspiring technician, a hobbyist, or a professional in the lighting industry, this guide will equip you with the knowledge and skills to tackle common issues and save money on repairs. Let's dive in!

CONTENTS

Chapter 1: Understanding PAR Lights or PAR can Lights

1.1 What are PAR Lights?

PAR lights, short for Parabolic Aluminized Reflector lights, are widely used in the entertainment industry, stage lighting, concerts, theatres, and architectural lighting. They are versatile lighting fixtures known for their ability to produce a focused and controllable beam of light.

PAR lights consist of a sealed metal housing with a parabolic reflector at the back and a lamp holder at the front. They are available in various sizes, such as PAR16, PAR20, PAR38, and PAR64, with each size offering different beam angles and light output capabilities.

These lights use a filament or a high-intensity discharge (HID) lamp as the light source. Filament-based PAR lamps usually utilise incandescent or halogen bulbs, while HID lamps include metal halide or high-pressure sodium bulbs.

PAR lights are popular due to their robust construction, versatility, and the ability to create vibrant and saturated colours using colour gels or colour filters. They are commonly used for stage lighting to highlight performers, create dramatic effects, or provide general illumination in different settings.

The reflector inside the PAR light housing helps control the beam angle and focus the light output. By adjusting the position of the lamp within the fixture or using accessories like barn doors or snoots, you can further shape and control the light beam's direction and spread.

PAR lights often have adjustable brackets or yokes that allow for easy mounting and positioning on lighting stands, trusses, or other support structures.

Understanding the basics of PAR lights is essential for troubleshooting and repairing common issues that may arise, such as bulb replacement, wiring problems, or issues with the internal reflector. In the following chapters, we will delve into the components, working principles, and repair techniques specific to PAR lights.

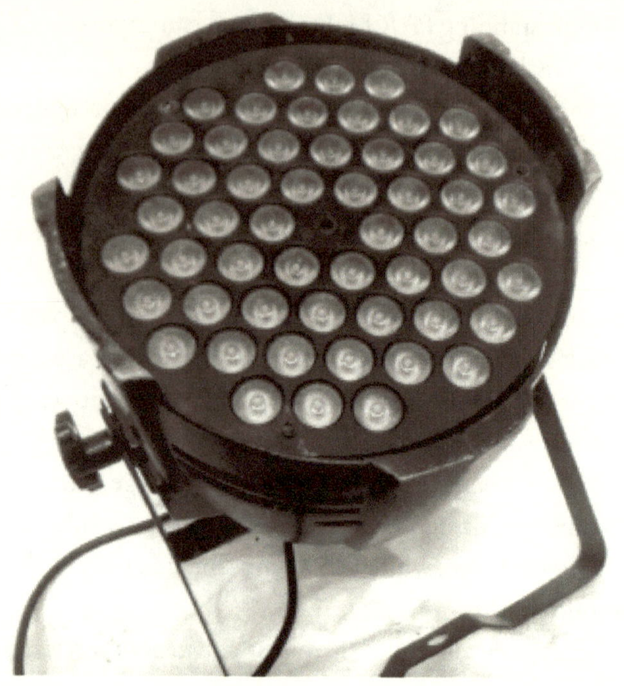

1.2 Components and Working Principle of PAR Lights

PAR lights consist of several key components that work together to produce and control the light output. Understanding these components is crucial for troubleshooting and repairing PAR lights effectively. Here are the main components and their functions:

1. Lamp: The lamp is the light source within the PAR light fixture. It can be an incandescent, halogen, or high-intensity discharge (HID) lamp, depending on the specific model. The lamp emits light when powered.

2. Reflector: The parabolic reflector is a curved surface located at the back of the PAR light. Its purpose is to gather and reflect the light emitted by the lamp. The shape of the reflector helps to focus the light into a beam and control its spread and intensity.

3. Lamp Holder: The lamp holder is the socket that holds the lamp in place within the PAR light fixture. It provides electrical connections to power the lamp and secure it in position.

4. Housing: The housing is the outer casing of the PAR light that encloses the lamp, reflector, and other internal components. It protects the internal components and provides structural support for the fixture.

5. Lens or Glass Cover: Some PAR lights feature a lens or glass cover at the front of the fixture. This transparent cover helps protect the lamp and reflector from dust, moisture, and damage. It may also have an impact on the beam angle and light diffusion.

6. Yoke or Bracket: The yoke or bracket is a component that allows the PAR light to be mounted and positioned. It provides flexibility in adjusting the angle and direction of the light beam. The yoke typically includes handles or knobs for easy adjustment and locking mechanisms to secure the fixture

in place.

Working Principle:

The working principle of PAR lights is relatively straightforward. When the lamp is powered, it emits light in various directions. The parabolic reflector inside the fixture gathers the light and reflects it forward, focusing it into a beam with a specific spread and intensity.

By adjusting the position of the lamp within the fixture or using accessories such as barn doors or snoots, the beam angle and direction can be modified. This allows for versatile lighting effects, including spot lighting, flood lighting, or highlighting specific areas or objects.

The reflector's shape and the lamp's position within the fixture play a significant role in controlling the light output. The combination of the lamp, reflector, and any additional accessories or modifiers determines the characteristics of the beam, such as its width, intensity, and colour.

Understanding the components and working principle of PAR lights provides a foundation for troubleshooting and repairing issues that may arise with these fixtures. In the following chapters, we will explore common issues, repair techniques, and maintenance tips specific to PAR lights.

1.3 Common Issues and Their Causes of PAR Lights

PAR lights, like any other lighting fixtures, can experience various issues that affect their performance. Understanding the common problems and their underlying causes can help you effectively troubleshoot and repair PAR lights. Here are some of the common issues you may encounter:

1. Dim or Flickering Light: If your PAR light is producing a dim or flickering light output, several factors could be responsible:

• Faulty Lamp: The lamp itself may be nearing the end of its lifespan or may have a loose connection. Consider replacing the lamp with a new one.

• Power Supply Issues: Check the power source and connections to ensure a stable power supply. Loose wiring or a faulty power outlet can cause inconsistent power delivery, resulting in dim or flickering light.

1. Uneven Light Distribution: Uneven light distribution can occur when the beam produced by the PAR light is not evenly spread across the intended area. Causes include:

• Misaligned Lamp: Ensure that the lamp is correctly positioned within the fixture and aligned with the reflector. A misaligned lamp can result in an uneven beam pattern.

• Dirty or Damaged Reflector: A dirty or damaged reflector can disrupt the light distribution. Clean the reflector gently using a non-abrasive cloth or replace it if necessary.

1. Overheating or Thermal Shutdown: PAR lights can generate heat, and if not properly managed, they may overheat or trigger

a thermal shutdown. Causes include:

● Poor Ventilation: Insufficient airflow around the fixture can lead to heat buildup. Ensure that the PAR light has proper ventilation and is not placed in enclosed spaces.

● High Ambient Temperature: Operating the PAR light in excessively high ambient temperatures can cause overheating. Consider using additional cooling measures, such as fans or heat sinks.

1. Loose or Damaged Wiring: Loose or damaged wiring can result in intermittent power supply, flickering, or complete failure of the PAR light. Check the wiring connections inside the fixture and ensure they are secure and free from damage. Replace any damaged wiring as needed.
2. Colour Inconsistencies: PAR lights that produce colour may experience inconsistencies in colour output. Possible causes include:

● Colour Filter Issues: If the PAR light uses colour filters, check for damage or dirt on the filters. Replace or clean them as necessary to ensure consistent colour output.

● Lamp Ageing: Over time, the colour characteristics of lamps can change, resulting in colour inconsistencies. Consider replacing the lamp if the colour deviation becomes significant.

It's important to note that these troubleshooting suggestions provide a general starting point, and the specific issues and their causes can vary depending on the PAR light model and design. Always refer to the manufacturer's guidelines and consult a professional if needed for complex repairs or issues beyond your expertise.

1.4 Tools and Equipment Needed for Repair of PAR Lights

Repairing PAR lights often requires a set of specific tools and equipment to effectively troubleshoot and fix common issues. Here are some essential tools and equipment you may need:

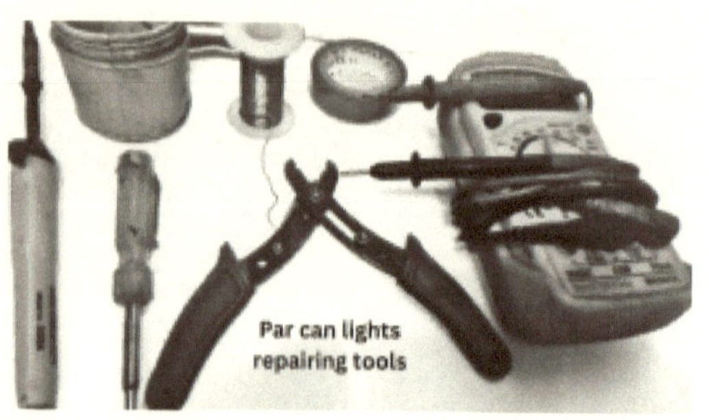

1. Screwdriver Set: A set of screwdrivers with different types and sizes (e.g., flathead, Phillips) is essential for accessing the internal components of the PAR light fixture.
2. Pliers: Pliers, such as needle-nose pliers and wire cutters, are useful for handling small components, bending wires, or cutting and stripping insulation from wires when necessary.
3. Multimeter: A multimeter is a versatile tool for measuring voltage, current, and resistance. It can help diagnose electrical issues, test connections, and verify continuity.
4. Soldering Iron and Solder: For repairing circuitry and replacing components, a soldering iron and solder are necessary. Choose a soldering iron with adjustable temperature control for versatility and use lead-free solder for safety.
5. Desoldering Tools: Desoldering tools like a desoldering pump or desoldering wick are helpful for removing solder from circuit boards when replacing faulty components.
6. Wire Strippers: Wire strippers allow you to remove the insulation from wires without damaging the underlying

conductors. Choose wire strippers suitable for the wire gauge commonly used in PAR lights.

7. Insulation Tape: Insulation tape or electrical tape is useful for insulating and protecting exposed wires or connections.

8. Cleaning Supplies: Cleaning the internal components of PAR lights can be necessary for maintenance or resolving issues related to dirt or corrosion. Non-abrasive cleaning solutions, lint-free cloth, and brushes can help with cleaning tasks.

9. Replacement Components: Depending on the specific issues you encounter, you may need replacement components such as lamps, reflectors, wiring connectors, or other electrical components. Ensure you have the appropriate replacements on hand.

10. Safety Equipment: When working with PAR lights or any electrical equipment, prioritise safety. Wear protective gear such as safety glasses and gloves to protect yourself from potential hazards.

Remember to refer to the manufacturer's documentation, guides, and safety precautions specific to your PAR light model. If you are unsure about any repair tasks or lack experience in working with electrical systems, it is advisable to seek professional assistance to avoid any safety risks or further damage to the fixture.

Chapter 2: Troubleshooting and Repairing PAR Lights

2.1 Safety Precautions

When working with PAR lights or any electrical equipment, it is crucial to prioritise safety to protect yourself and prevent accidents. Here are some essential safety precautions to follow when troubleshooting and repairing PAR lights:

1. Disconnect Power: Before starting any repair or maintenance work, always disconnect the PAR light from its power source. Unplug the fixture or turn off the circuit breaker to ensure that no electricity is flowing through the system.

2. Personal Protective Equipment (PPE): Wear appropriate personal protective equipment to safeguard yourself during repairs. This may include safety glasses, gloves, and non-conductive footwear. PPE helps protect against electrical shock, burns, and potential injury from broken glass or sharp components.

3. Work in a Well-Ventilated Area: Ensure that you are working in a well-ventilated space to prevent the buildup of heat, fumes, or potentially hazardous gases. Adequate ventilation helps maintain a comfortable and safe working environment.

4. Proper Lighting Conditions: Work in an area with sufficient lighting to clearly see the components and wiring of the PAR light. Good visibility reduces the risk of mistakes and potential accidents.

5. Familiarise Yourself with the PAR Light Model: Read and understand the manufacturer's documentation, including user manuals, technical specifications, and safety guidelines specific to the PAR light model you are working on. This will provide important information about the fixture's construction, electrical requirements, and any precautions specific to that model.

6. Avoid Working Alone: It is advisable to have someone present while you work on PAR lights, especially if you are performing tasks involving electrical connections or working at heights. A second person can assist in holding the fixture, handing tools, or providing help in case of an emergency.

7. Use Proper Tools and Equipment: Always use the appropriate tools and equipment for the task at hand. Using incorrect tools or makeshift solutions can lead to accidents, damage to the fixture, or ineffective repairs.

8. Avoid Water or Moisture: Keep PAR lights and your work area dry to prevent electrical shock and damage to the fixture. Avoid working on PAR lights in wet or damp conditions.

9. Follow Electrical Codes and Regulations: Adhere to local electrical codes and regulations when performing repairs on PAR lights. This ensures compliance with safety standards and minimises the risk of electrical hazards.

10. Seek Professional Help When Needed: If you are uncertain about any aspect of the repair process or encounter complex issues, it is recommended to seek assistance from a qualified professional or an authorised service centre. They have the expertise and experience to handle more advanced repairs and ensure safety.

By following these safety precautions, you can minimise risks and work effectively when troubleshooting and repairing PAR lights. Safety should always be the top priority to protect yourself and maintain the integrity of the lighting fixture.

2.2 Identifying Faulty Components of PAR Lights

When troubleshooting PAR lights, it is essential to identify faulty components accurately. Here are some common components that may cause issues and how to identify their faults:

1. Lamp: The lamp is the most common component to check when troubleshooting PAR lights. Look for signs such as a burned-out filament, discoloration, or visible damage. If the lamp appears faulty, replace it with a new one of the correct type and wattage.

2. Reflectors: Inspect the reflector for any cracks, dents, or discoloration. These issues can affect the light distribution and quality. If the reflector is damaged, it may need to be replaced with a new one.

3. Wiring and Connections: Faulty wiring or loose connections can cause issues with power supply and lead to dim or flickering light, or no light at all. Carefully inspect the wiring inside the fixture for any frayed, damaged, or disconnected wires. Check the connections between the lamp, socket, and other components to ensure they are secure and properly seated.

4. Sockets/Lamp Holders: Examine the lamp holders or sockets for signs of damage, such as broken or bent prongs or loose connections. Ensure that the lamp is properly seated and making good contact with the socket.

5. Power Supply and Control Circuitry: In cases where the PAR light has integrated control circuitry or electronic components, check for any visible damage or burnt-out components on the circuit boards. If there are issues with power supply or control, it may require advanced troubleshooting and repair by a qualified professional or authorised service centre.

6. External Accessories: If the PAR light has external accessories

like colour filters or barn doors, inspect them for damage, cracks, or wear. Damaged accessories may need to be replaced to maintain proper functionality.

When identifying faulty components, it is important to follow proper safety precautions, such as disconnecting the power source and wearing appropriate personal protective equipment. If you are unsure about any aspect of component identification or lack experience in working with electrical systems, it is advisable to consult a professional or an authorised service centre.

In the next section, we will explore troubleshooting techniques to help narrow down the causes of issues in PAR lights and further diagnose specific problems.

2.3 Soldering and Desoldering Techniques for PAR Lights

Soldering and desoldering are essential skills when it comes to repairing PAR lights. These techniques allow you to replace faulty components, repair broken connections, or modify circuitry. Here are some soldering and desoldering techniques commonly used for PAR lights:

Soldering Techniques:

1. Prepare the Work Area: Ensure you have a clean, well-lit workspace. Clear any clutter and make sure the PAR light is disconnected from the power source.

2. Choose the Right Soldering Iron and Tip: Select a soldering iron with an appropriate wattage for the task. A temperature-controlled iron with interchangeable tips is ideal. Use a tip size that matches the size of the component or connection you are soldering.

3. Heat the Soldering Iron: Plug in the soldering iron and allow it to heat up to the desired temperature. Wait until the soldering iron reaches its operating temperature before proceeding.

4. Clean and Tin the Iron Tip: Before soldering, clean the soldering iron tip with a damp sponge or brass tip cleaner to remove any residue or oxidation. Then, apply a small amount of solder to the tip (tinning) to help with heat transfer and improve soldering efficiency.

5. Flux Application: Apply flux to the area you plan to solder. Flux helps improve solder flow and creates a clean solder joint. Use a small amount and spread it evenly with a flux pen or brush.

6. Heat the Connection: Place the heated soldering iron tip on the component lead and the pad or wire you want to solder. Heat the connection for a few seconds to ensure proper heat transfer.

7. Apply Solder: Once the connection is heated, touch the solder wire to the joint. Allow the solder to flow onto the connection, creating a smooth and shiny solder joint. Use the right amount of solder—too little may result in a weak joint, while too much can cause solder bridges or shorts.

8. Remove Heat: After applying solder, remove the soldering iron and continue to hold the joint steady until the solder solidifies. Avoid moving or disturbing the joint until it cools down.

Desoldering Techniques:

1. Prepare the Work Area: As with soldering, ensure you have a clean and well-lit workspace. Disconnect the PAR light from the power source.

2. Choose the Right Desoldering Tools: There are two commonly used desoldering techniques: desoldering pumps (also known as solder suckers) and desoldering wicks. Both tools are effective for removing solder from joints.

3. Heat the Solder: Heat the solder joint with a soldering iron, focusing on the area you want to remove the solder from. Apply heat until the solder becomes molten.

4. Desoldering Pump: Position the desoldering pump near the molten solder and press the plunger. The pump will create a vacuum that sucks up the molten solder. Keep the tip of the desoldering pump close to the joint for optimal results.

5. Desoldering Wick: Alternatively, you can use a desoldering wick (also called solder wick) to remove molten solder. Place the desoldering wick on the molten solder and press it against the joint with the heated soldering iron. The wick absorbs the solder through capillary action.

6. Clean the Area: Once the solder is removed, clean the area with isopropyl alcohol or a flux cleaner to remove any residual flux or debris.

Remember to practise proper safety precautions during soldering and desoldering, including using appropriate personal protective equipment, working in a well-ventilated area.

2.4 Replacing Faulty Components of PAR Lights

In the process of repairing PAR lights, there may be instances where you need to replace faulty components. Here are the general steps to follow when replacing components in PAR lights:

1. Identify the Faulty Component: Through the troubleshooting process, determine which specific component needs to be replaced. It could be a lamp, reflector, socket, wiring, or any other part contributing to the issue.

2. Prepare the Work Area: Ensure you have a clean and well-lit workspace. Disconnect the PAR light from the power source to prevent any accidental electrical shock.

3. Gather the Replacement Component: Obtain the appropriate replacement component that matches the specifications of the faulty part. Refer to the manufacturer's documentation or consult with a supplier to ensure compatibility.

4. Disassemble the PAR Light: Depending on the design of the PAR light, you may need to disassemble the fixture to access the faulty component. Use the necessary tools, such as screwdrivers or pliers, to remove any screws, clips, or fasteners holding the fixture together. Take note of the disassembly process and keep track of the removed parts to ensure proper reassembly later.

5. Remove the Faulty Component: Once you have access to the faulty component, carefully disconnect it from the PAR light. This may involve unscrewing, unplugging, or desoldering the component, depending on its type and connection method. Take care not to damage any surrounding components or wiring during removal.

6. Install the Replacement Component: Take the new component and connect it in place of the faulty one. Ensure that the connections are secure, wires are properly seated, and

any necessary screws or fasteners are tightened. If soldering is required, follow proper soldering techniques mentioned earlier to establish a reliable and clean connection.

7. Reassemble the PAR Light: Once the replacement component is installed, reassemble the PAR light by reversing the disassembly steps. Ensure that all parts are correctly aligned and properly secured.

8. Test the PAR Light: After reassembly, reconnect the PAR light to the power source and test its functionality. Check if the issue has been resolved and if the replaced component is working as expected. Verify that all connections are secure and that the PAR light operates safely.

Remember to refer to the manufacturer's guidelines and documentation specific to your PAR light model during the component replacement process. If you are unsure about any aspect of the repair or lack experience in working with electrical systems, it is advisable to seek assistance from a qualified professional or an authorised service centre.

2.5 Testing and Verifying Repairs of PAR Lights

Once you have completed the repair or replacement of components in PAR lights, it is crucial to test and verify that the repairs have been successful. Here are some steps to test and verify the functionality of PAR lights after repairs:

1. Power On the PAR Light: Connect the PAR light to a power source and turn it on. Ensure that the power source is compatible with the voltage requirements of the fixture.

2. Check for Proper Illumination: Observe the PAR light to see if it illuminates as expected. Note the brightness, colour, and overall quality of the light output. Pay attention to any flickering, dimming, or irregular behaviour that may indicate ongoing issues.

3. Test Different Modes and Settings: If the PAR light has various modes or settings, such as different colours, strobe effects, or dimming options, test each of them to ensure they are functioning correctly.

4. Verify Control and Connectivity: If the PAR light is controllable via DMX or other control protocols, check if it responds correctly to control signals. Test the connectivity and functionality of any control ports, buttons, or switches on the fixture.

5. Inspect Connections and Wiring: Visually inspect the repaired area and surrounding components to ensure that all connections are secure, wires are properly routed, and there are no loose or exposed wires. Make sure there are no signs of overheating or abnormal behaviour in the repaired section.

6. Perform Stress Tests: Depending on the nature of the repair, consider performing stress tests to validate the durability and reliability of the repaired PAR light. This may involve subjecting the fixture to extended periods of operation, varying

environmental conditions, or rigorous use to ensure that it can withstand normal operating conditions.

7. Seek Feedback: If possible, obtain feedback from end-users or clients who regularly use PAR lights in professional settings. They can provide valuable insights into the performance and functionality of the repaired fixture.

8. Document Repairs and Test Results: Keep a record of the repairs performed and the test results obtained. This documentation will be useful for future reference, warranty claims, or further troubleshooting if needed.

If you encounter any issues during the testing phase or if the repairs do not appear to have resolved the original problem, it may be necessary to reevaluate the repair process or seek assistance from a qualified professional or an authorised service centre.

Remember, safety should always be a priority when testing and operating PAR lights. Follow proper safety precautions, such as wearing personal protective equipment, working in a well-ventilated area, and ensuring the PAR light is properly grounded.

Chapter 3: 12V SMPS Repair

3.1 Introduction to 12V SMPS

Switched-Mode Power Supplies (SMPS) are widely used in various electronic devices to convert electrical power efficiently. A 12V SMPS, as the name suggests, is a power supply that provides a regulated output voltage of 12 volts. It is commonly used in applications such as computer systems, LED lighting, automotive electronics, and many other low-voltage devices.

The 12V SMPS operates by using high-frequency switching techniques to convert the input voltage (typically from the mains or a DC source) to a stable 12V output. It consists of several key components and stages that work together to achieve efficient power conversion:

1. Rectification Stage: The AC input voltage is first rectified using diodes to convert it into a pulsating DC voltage.
2. Filter Stage: A capacitor or an inductor is used to smooth the pulsating DC voltage and reduce ripple.
3. Power Switching Stage: This stage involves a power switch (typically a MOSFET or transistor) that rapidly turns on and off to control the flow of current through an inductor or transformer.
4. Transformer Stage: The switching action of the power switch allows the voltage to be stepped up or stepped down using a

transformer, depending on the desired output voltage.

5. Rectification and Filtering of Output: The transformed voltage is rectified and filtered again to obtain a stable DC output voltage close to 12V.

6. Voltage Regulation: A feedback circuit monitors the output voltage and adjusts the duty cycle of the power switch to maintain a steady 12V output despite changes in input voltage or load conditions.

While 12V SMPSs are generally reliable, they can develop faults over time or due to various factors such as power surges, component ageing, or environmental conditions. Understanding how to troubleshoot and repair these issues is crucial for maintaining the functionality of the power supply.

In the following sections, we will explore common issues that can occur in 12V SMPS units, their possible causes, and techniques for troubleshooting and repairing them effectively.

3.2 Common Problems with 12V SMPS

Like any electronic device, 12V SMPS units can experience various problems. Understanding the common issues that can occur will help you diagnose and repair them effectively. Here are some common problems you may encounter with 12V SMPS units:

1. No Output Voltage: One of the most common problems is when the 12V SMPS fails to provide any output voltage. This can be caused by issues such as a blown fuse, faulty rectifier diodes, defective power switch, or a malfunctioning feedback circuit.

2. Overheating: Overheating can occur due to a variety of reasons, including insufficient cooling, excessive load, or faulty components such as capacitors, transformers, or the power switch. Excessive heat can lead to thermal shutdown or component failure if not addressed.

3. Voltage Instability: If the output voltage fluctuates or deviates from the desired 12V, it can cause issues with the devices powered by the SMPS. This may be due to problems with the voltage regulation circuit, feedback loop, or faulty components such as capacitors or resistors.

4. High Ripple Current: Ripple refers to the AC component present in the DC output of the SMPS. If the ripple current is too high, it can cause interference in connected devices or affect their performance. Common causes of high ripple current include defective capacitors, improper filtering, or issues with the rectification stage.

5. Strange Noises: Unusual noises, such as buzzing or humming, coming from the 12V SMPS indicate a potential problem. These noises can be caused by loose components, faulty transformers, or improper grounding.

6. Intermittent Operation: When the 12V SMPS works

intermittently or powers off unexpectedly, it can be frustrating and indicate an underlying issue. This can be caused by loose connections, faulty solder joints, or thermal issues that cause components to malfunction under certain conditions.

7. Component Failure: Various components within the 12V SMPS, such as capacitors, diodes, transformers, or the power switch, can fail over time due to ageing, voltage surges, or excessive heat. Component failure can lead to a range of issues, including power loss, voltage irregularities, or complete unit failure.

In the next sections, we will discuss troubleshooting techniques and repair methods to address these common problems effectively. It's important to follow proper safety precautions and have a good understanding of electronics before attempting any repairs on the 12V SMPS. If you are unsure about any aspect of the repair process, consult a qualified technician or seek assistance from an authorised service centre.

3.3 Step-by-Step Troubleshooting Procedure

When encountering issues with a 12V SMPS, following a systematic troubleshooting procedure will help identify and resolve the problem effectively. Here is a step-by-step guide to troubleshooting a 12V SMPS:

1. Disconnect Power: Before starting any troubleshooting, disconnect the 12V SMPS from the power source to ensure your safety and prevent further damage to the unit.

2. Visual Inspection: Perform a visual inspection of the SMPS for any obvious signs of damage, loose connections, or burnt components. Check for any blown fuses, discoloured areas on the circuit board, or bulging capacitors. Make sure all components are properly seated and securely connected.

3. Test the Input Power: Verify the input power source to ensure it is within the specified range. Use a multimeter to measure the input voltage and check if it matches the expected range. If the input voltage is incorrect, the SMPS may not function properly.

4. Check Output Voltage: Connect the 12V SMPS to a load or use a multimeter to measure the output voltage. Compare the measured voltage with the desired 12V output. If there is no output voltage or if it deviates significantly from 12V, further troubleshooting is required.

5. Inspect Fuses and Protection Circuitry: Check the fuses in the SMPS for any signs of damage or blown fuses. Replace any blown fuses with the appropriate rating. Also, inspect the protection circuitry, such as over-current or over-temperature protection, and ensure they are functioning correctly.

6. Inspect Capacitors: Capacitor failure is a common issue in SMPS units. Check for any bulging or leaking capacitors on the circuit board. If you spot any defective capacitors, replace them with capacitors of the same capacitance and voltage

rating.

7. Test Diodes and Transistors: Diodes and transistors are essential components in the rectification and switching stages of the SMPS. Use a multimeter in diode mode to test them for proper functionality. Replace any faulty diodes or transistors as necessary.

8. Check Transformers and Inductors: Inspect transformers and inductors for any signs of damage, loose windings, or shorted windings. Use an ohmmeter to measure the resistance across the windings and ensure they are within the specified range. Replace any faulty transformers or inductors.

9. Verify Control and Feedback Circuitry: Check the control and feedback circuitry responsible for regulating the output voltage. Inspect components such as resistors, potentiometers, operational amplifiers, and optocouplers. Test these components using appropriate techniques, such as measuring resistance or voltage levels. Replace any faulty components.

10. Test the Power Switch: If the SMPS has a power switch, verify its functionality using a multimeter. Ensure it is turning on and off properly and allowing the correct flow of current through the SMPS.

11. Thermal Inspection: Check for any components that may be overheating. Use a thermal imaging camera or a non-contact infrared thermometer to identify hotspots. Excessive heat can lead to component failure or thermal shutdown. Improve cooling or address any thermal issues accordingly.

12. Reassemble and Retest: Once you have completed the necessary repairs or replacements, reassemble the SMPS and reconnect it to the power source. Test the functionality and stability of the 12V output voltage. Ensure that the repaired SMPS operates as expected.

Remember to exercise caution and follow safety guidelines when troubleshooting and repairing the 12V SMPS. If you are unsure about any step or lack experience in working with electronics, it is advisable to seek assistance.

3.4 Capacitor Replacement and Voltage Regulation

Capacitors are critical components in 12V SMPS units, and their failure can lead to various issues, including voltage instability, high ripple current, and power loss. In this section, we will discuss the process of replacing faulty capacitors and ensuring proper voltage regulation in the 12V SMPS.

1. Identify Faulty Capacitors: Begin by visually inspecting the capacitors on the SMPS circuit board. Look for any signs of bulging, leaking electrolyte, or discoloration. These are indications of capacitor failure. Additionally, use a capacitance metre or a multimeter with a capacitance measurement function to test the capacitance of each capacitor. Compare the measured capacitance with the manufacturer's specifications to identify capacitors that are out of tolerance.

2. Select Replacement Capacitors: Once you have identified faulty capacitors, procure suitable replacements. Ensure that the replacement capacitors have the same capacitance value (measured in microfarads, µF) and voltage rating as the original ones. It is generally recommended to use capacitors with the same or higher voltage rating to ensure reliability.

3. Safety Precautions: Before proceeding with capacitor replacement, disconnect the SMPS from the power source and discharge any stored energy in the capacitors. This can be done by shorting the capacitor terminals with a resistor or using a discharge tool. Capacitors can store high voltages even after the power is disconnected, so take precautions to avoid electrical shocks.

4. Desoldering Capacitors: Use a desoldering pump or desoldering braid to remove the faulty capacitors from the circuit board. Heat each solder joint connecting the capacitor leads to the board while gently pulling the component away.

Take care not to damage the surrounding components or the circuit board during this process.

5. Mounting and Soldering Replacement Capacitors: Insert the replacement capacitors into the appropriate positions on the circuit board, ensuring the correct polarity (positive and negative terminals). Align the capacitor leads with the corresponding solder pads. Apply heat to the solder pads while carefully soldering the capacitor leads, ensuring a secure and reliable connection. Trim any excess leads if necessary.

6. Voltage Regulation Adjustment: Some 12V SMPS units may have voltage regulation adjustment features. If the output voltage is not stable or deviates from the desired 12V, you may need to adjust the voltage regulation circuit. Consult the SMPS manufacturer's documentation or datasheet for specific instructions on voltage adjustment procedures. This may involve adjusting potentiometers or other voltage regulation components to achieve the desired output voltage.

7. Test and Verify: After replacing capacitors and adjusting voltage regulation, reconnect the 12V SMPS to the power source and test the output voltage using a multimeter. Ensure that the output voltage remains stable at 12V within an acceptable tolerance range. Monitor for any signs of voltage fluctuations or irregularities.

It's important to note that the process of replacing capacitors and adjusting voltage regulation requires a certain level of knowledge and skill in electronics. If you are uncertain about any step or lack experience, it is advisable to seek assistance from a qualified technician or an authorised service centre.

3.5 Testing the Repaired 12V SMPS

After performing repairs on a 12V SMPS, it is crucial to thoroughly test the unit to ensure that it is functioning correctly and providing stable output voltage. Here are the steps to test the repaired 12V SMPS:

1. Safety Precautions: Before testing the SMPS, ensure that all connections are secure and follow appropriate safety precautions. Disconnect the SMPS from the power source and discharge any stored energy in capacitors as per the safety guidelines provided earlier.

2. Visual Inspection: Conduct a visual inspection of the repaired SMPS. Check for any loose connections, misplaced components, or soldering defects. Verify that all replaced components are of the correct value and properly installed.

3. Reconnect the SMPS: Connect the repaired 12V SMPS to a load or a test circuit. Ensure that the input and output connections are correctly established. Double-check the polarity of the connections to prevent damage to the SMPS or connected devices.

4. Power On: Reconnect the SMPS to the power source and turn it on. Observe any initial startup behaviour, such as the cooling fan spinning or LED indicators lighting up. Listen for any abnormal noises, such as buzzing or humming, which could indicate potential issues.

5. Output Voltage Measurement: Use a multimeter to measure the output voltage of the repaired 12V SMPS. Connect the multimeter probes to the positive and negative output terminals of the SMPS. Verify that the measured voltage is stable and within the desired 12V range. Monitor the voltage for any fluctuations or deviations.

6. Load Testing: Apply a load to the 12V SMPS to simulate real-world operating conditions. This can be done by connecting

appropriate resistors or electronic devices that draw a sufficient current. Monitor the output voltage while the load is applied and ensure that it remains stable and within the acceptable tolerance range.

7. Ripple Current Measurement: Use an oscilloscope or a multimeter with an AC voltage measurement function to measure the ripple current in the output voltage. Connect the measuring device across the output terminals and observe the waveform. Ensure that the ripple current is within acceptable limits specified by the SMPS manufacturer.

8. Thermal Testing: Monitor the temperature of critical components, such as transformers, power switches, and heat sinks, during operation. Use a thermal imaging camera or a non-contact infrared thermometer to identify any hotspots or excessive heat. Ensure that the repaired SMPS does not overheat and maintains a safe operating temperature.

9. Longevity Testing: Run the repaired 12V SMPS for an extended period to assess its long-term stability and reliability. Monitor the output voltage, temperature, and overall performance during this testing phase. Note any abnormalities or issues that may arise during extended operation.

10. Final Verification: After completing the testing process, evaluate the performance of the repaired 12V SMPS against the desired specifications. Ensure that it meets the required output voltage, stability, and efficiency standards. If any issues or deviations are observed, revisit the troubleshooting and repair process to address them accordingly.

By following these testing steps, you can verify the effectiveness of the repairs performed on the 12V SMPS and ensure its proper functioning. If you encounter persistent issues or are unsure about the testing process, it is recommended to seek assistance from a qualified technician or an authorised service centre.

Chapter 4: 5V SMPS Repair

4.1 Understanding 5V SMPS

In this chapter, we will delve into the world of 5V Switched-Mode Power Supplies (SMPS). A 5V SMPS is a type of power supply that converts the input voltage to a stable 5V output voltage, which is commonly used to power various electronic devices and components.

1. Working Principle: The working principle of a 5V SMPS is similar to other SMPS units. It uses a switching regulator circuit to convert the input voltage (typically from an AC source or a higher DC voltage) to a 5V DC output voltage. The switching regulator employs high-frequency switching to control the voltage conversion process efficiently.

2. Components: A 5V SMPS consists of various components that work together to regulate the output voltage. These components include:

a. Transformer: The transformer is responsible for isolating and stepping down the input voltage to a suitable level for further processing.

b. Rectification Circuit: The rectification circuit converts the AC input voltage to a pulsating DC voltage.

c. Filtering Circuit: The filtering circuit removes the unwanted AC ripples and smoothens the rectified DC voltage.

d. Switching Regulator: The switching regulator controls the switching process and adjusts the duty cycle to regulate the output voltage at 5V.

e. Feedback Circuit: The feedback circuit senses the output voltage and provides feedback to the switching regulator, enabling it to maintain a stable 5V output.

f. Capacitors, Diodes, and Inductors: These components are essential for smoothing the output voltage, filtering noise, and regulating the current flow within the SMPS.

3. Applications: 5V SMPS units find widespread applications in various electronic devices and systems, including:

a. Consumer Electronics: Many consumer electronics devices such as smartphones, tablets, gaming consoles, and audio/video equipment require a 5V power supply.

b. Embedded Systems: Microcontrollers, development boards, and other embedded systems often operate at 5V and rely on 5V SMPS units for power.

c. IoT Devices: Internet of Things (IoT) devices and sensors often use 5V power supplies due to their low power requirements.

d. USB Power Supplies: USB chargers and power adapters provide a 5V output to charge smartphones, tablets, and other USB-powered devices.

e. Computer Peripherals: Various computer peripherals, including external hard drives, keyboards, mice, and USB hubs, utilise 5V power supplies.

Understanding the basics of 5V SMPS is crucial for effectively troubleshooting and repairing any issues that may arise. In the subsequent sections, we will explore common problems, troubleshooting techniques, and repair methods specific to 5V SMPS units.

4.2 Common Issues and Troubleshooting Techniques of 5V SMPS Repair

5V SMPS units can experience various issues that affect their performance and output voltage stability. In this section, we will explore common problems encountered in 5V SMPS units and discuss troubleshooting techniques to identify and resolve these issues effectively.

1. No Output Voltage or Low Output Voltage:

• Check the input power source to ensure it is supplying the correct voltage.

• Inspect the rectification circuit for any faulty diodes or bridge rectifiers.

• Verify the transformer for any open or shorted windings.

• Test the output capacitors for proper capacitance and ESR (Equivalent Series Resistance).

• Check the feedback circuit and ensure it is providing the correct feedback to the switching regulator.

1. High Output Voltage or Voltage Fluctuations:

• Check the feedback circuit and ensure it is functioning correctly.

• Inspect the voltage regulation circuitry, including voltage reference components and feedback resistors.

• Verify the stability of the switching regulator circuit and its components, such as transistors and ICs.

- Test the output capacitors for proper capacitance and voltage rating.

- Ensure that the load connected to the 5V SMPS is within the specified limits.

1. Overheating or Thermal Shutdown:

- Inspect the heat sink and cooling system for any obstructions or dust accumulation.

- Verify the functionality of the cooling fan and ensure it is operating properly.

- Check for any shortened or faulty components that may be causing excessive heat generation.

- Monitor the temperature of critical components using a thermal imaging camera or a non-contact infrared thermometer.

1. Excessive Ripple or Noise in Output:

- Inspect the output filtering capacitors for any signs of degradation or high ESR.

- Check for loose or damaged components that may be introducing noise into the circuit.

- Ensure proper grounding of the SMPS and the connected devices.

- Add additional filtering components, such as inductors or ferrite beads, to suppress noise.

1. Protection Circuit Activation or Shutdown Issues:

• Verify the functionality of the over-current, over-voltage, and over-temperature protection circuitry.

• Check for shorted components or excessive current draw from the load.

• Inspect the protection circuit components, such as fuses and current-sensing resistors, for any faults or open circuits.

• Ensure that the protection circuit is properly configured and calibrated.

Troubleshooting these issues requires a systematic approach, including visual inspections, component testing, and circuit analysis. Use appropriate tools such as a multimeter, oscilloscope, and thermal imaging camera to aid in the troubleshooting process. It is important to refer to the SMPS manufacturer's documentation and datasheets for specific troubleshooting guidelines and circuit diagrams.

Remember to take necessary safety precautions when working with 5V SMPS units, such as disconnecting power sources, discharging capacitors, and following proper handling procedures. If you are unsure about any step or lack experience in working with electronics, it is advisable to seek assistance from a qualified technician or an authorised service centre.

4.3 Diagnosing and Fixing Short Circuits in 5V SMPS Repair

Short circuits are a common problem in 5V SMPS units that can lead to power supply failure, overheating, or even damage to connected devices. It is crucial to diagnose and fix short circuits promptly to ensure the safe and proper functioning of the SMPS. In this section, we will discuss the steps involved in diagnosing and fixing short circuits in 5V SMPS units.

1. Visual Inspection: Perform a visual inspection of the circuit board and components. Look for any signs of burnt or melted components, damaged traces, or abnormal discoloration. Pay close attention to areas where components may come into contact with each other or with the circuit board.

2. Disconnection: Disconnect the 5V SMPS from the power source to ensure your safety and prevent further damage.

3. Component Testing: Use a multimeter to test individual components for short circuits. Start by setting the multimeter to the resistance (ohms) mode. Place one probe on the component's positive lead or pin and the other probe on the negative lead or pin. If the multimeter shows a very low resistance reading (close to zero ohms), it indicates a short circuit in that component.

4. Isolation: Once a shorted component is identified, isolate it from the circuit board by desoldering its leads or pins. This will allow you to test the remaining circuit without interference from the shorted component.

5. Trace Inspection: Inspect the circuit board traces near the isolated component for any visible signs of damage, such as burns, breaks, or cuts. Use a magnifying glass if necessary. Traces can get damaged due to excessive current flow or overheating caused by the short circuit.

6. Continuity Testing: Set the multimeter to the continuity or

beep mode. Place one probe on one end of a trace connected to the isolated component and the other probe on the other end. If the multimeter beeps or shows continuity, it indicates that the trace is intact. If there is no beep or continuity, there may be a break or damage in the trace.

7. Trace Repair: If you find a damaged or broken trace, you can repair it using a copper wire or conductive ink. Carefully scrape off any protective coating from the trace and solder the copper wire across the break, ensuring a secure connection. If using conductive ink, carefully apply it over the damaged trace and let it dry as per the manufacturer's instructions.

8. Component Replacement: If the shorted component is irreparable or cannot be easily replaced, such as an integrated circuit (IC), you may need to replace it with a new component. Ensure that the replacement component matches the specifications and pin configuration of the original component.

9. Reassembly and Testing: Once the short circuit has been fixed, reassemble the 5V SMPS, reconnect it to the power source, and test its functionality. Measure the output voltage, check for abnormal heat, and monitor the SMPS's operation for any signs of further issues or short circuits.

Remember to take appropriate safety precautions throughout the repair process, such as wearing antistatic wristbands, working in a well-ventilated area, and following electrical safety guidelines.

If you encounter difficulties in diagnosing or fixing short circuits in a 5V SMPS or lack experience in working with electronics, it is advisable to seek assistance from a qualified technician or an authorised service centre.

4.4 Replacing Damaged Components in 5V SMPS Repair

In the process of repairing a 5V SMPS, it is common to come across damaged components that need to be replaced. Whether due to a short circuit, overheating, or general wear and tear, replacing faulty components is crucial for restoring the functionality and reliability of the SMPS. In this section, we will discuss the steps involved in replacing damaged components in a 5V SMPS.

1. Identify the Faulty Component: Before replacing any component, identify the specific component that is causing the issue. This can be done through visual inspection, component testing, or circuit analysis. Look for signs of physical damage, burnt marks, or abnormal readings on multimeter tests.

2. Gather Replacement Components: Once the faulty component is identified, obtain a replacement component with the same specifications. This includes the correct part number, package type, voltage and current ratings, and other relevant specifications. Ensure the replacement component is compatible with the 5V SMPS circuit.

3. Power Off and Discharge Capacitors: Before starting the replacement process, disconnect the 5V SMPS from the power source and discharge any stored energy in the capacitors. This is important for your safety and to prevent any accidental damage to the components.

4. Remove the Faulty Component: Using appropriate desoldering techniques, remove the faulty component from the circuit board. This typically involves applying heat to the solder joints while gently lifting the component with a desoldering tool or soldering iron. Be careful not to damage the circuit board or adjacent components.

5. Clean the Solder Pads: After removing the faulty component, clean the solder pads on the circuit board using a solder wick or

a desoldering pump. Ensure that the pads are free from excess solder or debris, allowing for proper soldering of the replacement component.

6. Prepare the Replacement Component: If necessary, trim the leads of the replacement component to the appropriate length. Make sure the leads are correctly oriented according to the component's polarity, if applicable. Bend the leads slightly to hold the component in place during soldering.

7. Solder the Replacement Component: Position the replacement component on the solder pads, aligning the leads with the corresponding pads on the circuit board. Apply heat to the solder pads while simultaneously touching the solder wire to create a good solder joint. Be mindful of not overheating the component or the circuit board.

8. Trim Excess Leads and Inspect: Once the replacement component is soldered in place, trim any excess lead length. Inspect the solder joints to ensure they are properly formed, shiny, and without any solder bridges or cold joints. Use a magnifying glass if needed for closer inspection.

9. Test the Repaired 5V SMPS: Reconnect the 5V SMPS to the power source and perform thorough testing. Measure the output voltage to ensure it is stable and within the desired range. Monitor the SMPS's operation for any abnormal behaviour or signs of further issues.

10. Finalise the Repair: If the repaired 5V SMPS is functioning correctly and providing the desired output voltage, reassemble any disassembled components or covers. Double-check all connections and ensure everything is securely in place.

Replacing damaged components in a 5V SMPS requires precision and attention to detail. If you are unfamiliar with soldering or lack experience in working with electronics, it is recommended to seek assistance from a qualified technician or an authorised service centre.

4.5 Verifying the 5V SMPS Repair

After completing the repair process for a 5V SMPS, it is essential to verify the repair to ensure that the SMPS is functioning properly and providing the desired output voltage. Verification helps confirm the effectiveness of the repair and provides confidence in the reliability of the repaired SMPS. In this section, we will discuss the steps involved in verifying the repair of a 5V SMPS.

1. Power Off and Safety Precautions: Before conducting any verification tests, make sure the 5V SMPS is powered off and disconnected from the power source. Take necessary safety precautions, such as wearing protective gloves and grounding yourself to avoid electrostatic discharge.

2. Visual Inspection: Perform a thorough visual inspection of the repaired SMPS. Check for any loose connections, soldering issues, or physical damage that might have been missed during the repair process. Ensure that all components are properly seated and secured.

3. Output Voltage Measurement: Use a multimeter or a suitable voltage measuring device to measure the output voltage of the repaired 5V SMPS. Connect the positive probe of the multimeter to the positive output terminal of the SMPS and the negative probe to the negative output terminal. Verify that the measured voltage is close to the desired 5V output, with acceptable tolerances.

4. Load Testing: Connect a load to the output terminals of the 5V SMPS to simulate the actual operating conditions. This can be a resistive load or an appropriate electronic device that requires a 5V power supply. Monitor the voltage stability under load and ensure that it remains within the specified range.

5. Ripple and Noise Measurement: Use an oscilloscope or a

dedicated ripple metre to measure the ripple and noise levels in the output voltage of the repaired SMPS. Check that the measured ripple and noise levels are within the acceptable limits specified by the SMPS manufacturer or industry standards.

6. Temperature Monitoring: During the load testing, monitor the temperature of critical components, such as the transformer, switching transistors, and heatsinks. Use a thermal imaging camera or a non-contact infrared thermometer to identify any abnormal temperature rise. Ensure that the temperature remains within safe operating limits and does not indicate excessive heat buildup.

7. Functional Testing: Perform functional testing of any protection circuits, such as over-current, over-voltage, and thermal protection. Ensure that these protection mechanisms are operating correctly and triggering as intended under abnormal operating conditions.

8. Operational Stability: Monitor the repaired 5V SMPS for a reasonable period of time under normal operating conditions. Check for any signs of instability, voltage fluctuations, or abnormal behaviour. Ensure that the SMPS continues to provide a stable and reliable 5V output.

9. Documentation and Reporting: Maintain proper documentation of the repair process, including the identified issues, steps taken for repair, replaced components, and verification results. This documentation can be useful for future reference or if the repaired SMPS requires further maintenance or troubleshooting.

By following these verification steps, you can confidently ensure that the repair of the 5V SMPS has been successful. If any issues or abnormalities are detected during the verification process, review the repair steps and consult relevant technical resources or seek assistance from a qualified technician or an authorised service centre.

Chapter 5: Pixel LED Systems Repair

5.1 Introduction to Pixel LED Systems

Pixel LED systems, also known as pixel mapping or pixel control systems, are lighting systems that consist of individual LED pixels arranged in a matrix or grid formation. These systems offer versatile and dynamic lighting effects, allowing for the creation of intricate patterns, animations, and colour displays. In this chapter, we will explore the fundamentals of pixel LED systems, their components, and how to repair common issues that may arise.

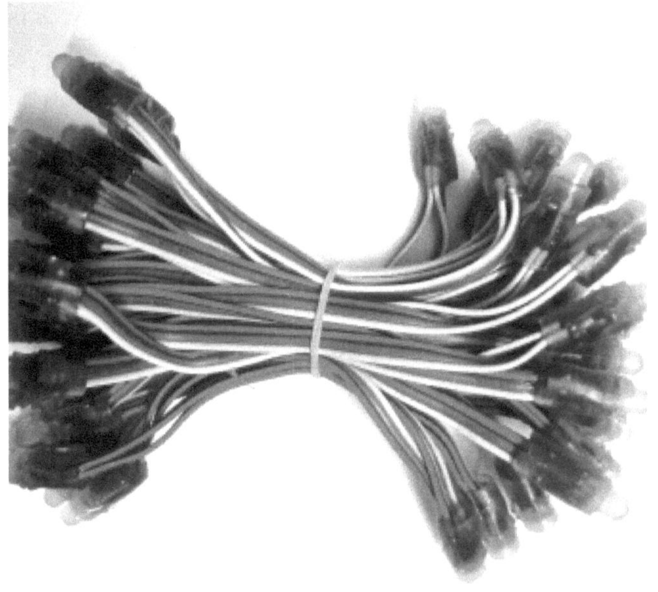

1. Understanding Pixel LED Systems: Pixel LED systems utilise addressable LEDs, where each individual LED pixel can be controlled independently. This level of control enables the creation of captivating visual effects and animations. Pixel LED systems are commonly used in stage lighting, architectural lighting, displays, and various other applications where

dynamic lighting is desired.

2. Components of Pixel LED Systems: A typical pixel LED system comprises the following components:

a. LED Pixels: These are individual LEDs arranged in a matrix or grid pattern. Each pixel usually contains multiple RGB (Red, Green, Blue) LEDs or RGBW (Red, Green, Blue, White) LEDs, allowing for a wide range of colour mixing possibilities.

b. LED Controllers: The LED controllers are responsible for sending control signals to the LED pixels. They receive input data, such as DMX or Art-Net, and translate it into commands that determine the colour, intensity, and behaviour of each pixel.

c. Power Supplies: Pixel LED systems require dedicated power supplies to provide the necessary voltage and current for the LEDs. The power supplies must be capable of handling the total power consumption of the system.

d. Control Software/Interface: To program and control the pixel LED system, specialised software or interfaces are used. These tools allow users to create and customise lighting effects, sequences, and animations.

3. Common Issues with Pixel LED Systems: Like any complex lighting system, pixel LED systems may encounter various issues over time. Some common problems include:

a. Faulty Pixels: Individual LED pixels may fail, resulting in flickering, incorrect colours, or complete non-functionality. This can be due to damaged LEDs, faulty connections, or issues with the LED driver circuitry.

b. Data Communication Problems: Issues in the data communication between the LED controller and the LED pixels can lead to incorrect colour output, inconsistent brightness, or synchronisation problems.

c. Power-related Issues: Insufficient power supply capacity, inadequate power distribution, or voltage fluctuations can cause improper functioning of the LED pixels, such as dimming, colour shifts, or intermittent operation.

d. Wiring and Connection Problems: Loose connections, damaged cables, or improper wiring can result in signal loss, erratic behaviour, or non-responsive pixels.

4. Troubleshooting and Repairing Pixel LED Systems: When troubleshooting and repairing pixel LED systems, it is crucial to follow these general steps:

a. Visual Inspection: Perform a visual inspection of the entire system, checking for any visible damage, loose connections, or signs of malfunctioning components.

b. Testing Individual Pixels: Test individual LED pixels using a multimeter or a pixel tester. Identify and replace any faulty pixels as necessary.

c. Data and Power Checks: Verify the integrity of the data signal and power supply. Test the LED controller's output signals and measure the voltage and current at different points in the system.

d. Connection Checks: Inspect and reseat all connections, ensuring they are secure and properly aligned. Repair or replace any damaged cables or connectors.

e. Firmware and Software Updates: Check for firmware or software updates for the LED controller and apply them if available. Software issues can sometimes cause unexpected behaviour or malfunctioning of the system.

f. Documentation and Record-keeping: Maintain detailed documentation of the troubleshooting process.

5.2 Troubleshooting Pixel Issues

Pixel LED systems can experience various issues that affect the proper functioning of individual pixels or groups of pixels. Troubleshooting these issues requires a systematic approach to identify and resolve the underlying problems. In this section, we will discuss the steps involved in troubleshooting pixel issues in a pixel LED system.

1. Observe the Symptoms: Start by observing the symptoms exhibited by the pixel LED system. Look for patterns of malfunctioning pixels, such as flickering, incorrect colours, or complete non-functionality. Note any specific areas or sections of the system that are affected.

2. Check Power Supply: Verify that the power supply to the pixel LED system is stable and supplying the correct voltage and current. Measure the voltage at various points in the system to ensure it is within the specified range. Insufficient power can lead to dimming or erratic behaviour of the pixels.

3. Inspect Data Connections: Examine the data connections between the LED controller and the pixels. Ensure that the cables and connectors are properly seated and secure. Check for any signs of damage or loose connections. Consider using a cable tester or continuity tester to confirm the integrity of the data signal.

4. Test Individual Pixels: Test individual pixels to identify any faulty units. This can be done using a multimeter or a pixel tester. Check for continuity, proper voltage readings, and colour output. Replace any defective pixels with new ones of the same specifications.

5. Address Signal Issues: If specific areas or sections of the pixel LED system exhibit issues, focus on troubleshooting the data signal in those areas. Check for proper signal transmission from the LED controller and verify that the data is reaching

the affected pixels.

6. Verify Controller Configuration: Review the configuration settings of the LED controller. Ensure that the correct protocol, addressing, and colour settings are configured for the pixel LED system. Incorrect configurations can result in erratic behaviour or incorrect colour output.

7. Check Grounding and EMI Interference: Poor grounding or electromagnetic interference (EMI) can affect the performance of the pixel LED system. Verify that the system is properly grounded and that there are no sources of EMI nearby. Consider using shielded cables or ferrite beads to mitigate interference.

8. Update Firmware and Software: Check for firmware or software updates for the LED controller. Upgrading to the latest version can address software-related issues and improve system performance. Follow the manufacturer's instructions for updating the firmware or software.

9. Document Findings: Maintain detailed documentation of the troubleshooting process, including the observed symptoms, tests conducted, and the solutions implemented. This documentation will be valuable for future reference and troubleshooting purposes.

If the troubleshooting process does not resolve the pixel issues, consider consulting the manufacturer's technical support or seeking assistance from an experienced technician or service centre specialised in pixel LED systems.

5.3 Dealing with Dead Pixels

Dead pixels are individual pixels in a pixel LED system that fail to illuminate or display any colour. They can be a common issue in pixel LED systems and can detract from the overall visual quality of the display. In this section, we will discuss how to identify and address dead pixels in a pixel LED system.

1. Identifying Dead Pixels: Dead pixels can be visually identified as individual pixels that do not light up or display any colour when the system is powered on. They may appear as black or non-responsive pixels amidst an otherwise functioning display.

2. Pixel Mapping and Documentation: Before attempting to repair dead pixels, it is crucial to have an accurate pixel map or documentation of the system's layout. This information will help pinpoint the exact location of the dead pixels and facilitate their replacement or repair.

3. Testing and Confirmation: Use a pixel tester or a multimeter to confirm that the suspected dead pixels are indeed not functioning. Test the voltage, continuity, and colour output of the pixels to verify their status.

4. Replacing Dead Pixels: Dead pixels can often be replaced with new working pixels of the same specifications. Follow these steps to replace dead pixels:

   a. Disconnect Power: Ensure the pixel LED system is powered off and disconnected from the power source before attempting any repairs.

   b. Remove Surrounding Pixels: If the dead pixel is surrounded by other pixels, carefully remove the surrounding pixels to gain access to the dead pixel. Use appropriate tools and techniques to avoid damaging adjacent pixels or the surrounding circuitry.

   c. Desolder Dead Pixel: Use a soldering iron and desoldering tools to remove the dead pixel from the circuit board. Take care not to overheat the circuit board or adjacent components during the desoldering process.

d. Install New Pixel: Insert a new working pixel of the same type and specifications in place of the dead pixel. Ensure proper alignment and orientation of the new pixel. Solder the connections carefully, following best soldering practices.

e. Test and Verify: After replacing the dead pixel, reconnect power to the pixel LED system and test the repaired pixel. Confirm that the new pixel functions correctly and displays the desired colors.

f. Replace Surrounding Pixels: If necessary, reattach the surrounding pixels that were removed earlier, ensuring proper alignment and soldering connections.

5. Documentation and Quality Assurance: Maintain documentation of the dead pixel replacement process, including the replaced pixel's location, specifications, and any other relevant details. This documentation will aid in future maintenance and troubleshooting.

It's important to note that the replacement of dead pixels requires soldering skills and knowledge of the pixel LED system's circuitry. If you are unsure or uncomfortable with performing the repairs yourself, it is advisable to seek assistance from a qualified technician or an authorised service centre specialising in pixel LED systems.

5.4 Power Injection and Data Signal Correction

Pixel LED systems may encounter issues related to power distribution and data signal integrity, which can lead to inconsistent colour output, brightness variations, or non-functioning pixels. Power injection and data signal correction techniques can help address these problems and ensure optimal performance of the pixel LED system. In this section, we will discuss power injection and data signal correction in pixel LED systems repair.

1. Power Injection: a. Understanding Power Injection: Power injection involves adding additional power sources at specific points in the pixel LED system to compensate for voltage drop and ensure consistent power supply to the pixels.

   b. Identifying Power Injection Points: Determine the locations where power injection is needed based on the length of the LED strip or the layout of the pixel LED system. These points are typically where the voltage drop is significant due to long cable runs or high power consumption.

   c. Calculating Power Requirements: Calculate the additional power needed for the power injection by considering the LED strip's power consumption and the distance from the power supply. Refer to the manufacturer's specifications or consult a power injection guide for accurate calculations.

   d. Adding Power Injection Connections: Connect additional power wires from the power supply to the designated power injection points. Ensure proper wire gauge and secure connections. Distribute the power evenly across the system to minimise voltage drop.

2. Data Signal Correction: a. Understanding Data Signal Correction: Data signal correction techniques are used to resolve issues related to data transmission and reception, ensuring accurate and consistent control of the pixel LEDs.

b. Signal Amplification: In cases where the data signal weakens over long cable runs, use signal amplifiers or repeaters to boost the signal strength. These devices help maintain the integrity of the data signal by amplifying weak signals and extending their reach.

c. Differential Signalling: Implement differential signalling techniques, such as using twisted pair cables or differential signal converters, to improve noise immunity and reduce signal interference. This helps minimise data errors and ensures reliable communication between the LED controller and the pixel LEDs.

d. Signal Termination: Properly terminate the data signal lines to prevent signal reflections and maintain signal integrity. Use termination resistors or termination techniques recommended by the LED controller manufacturer.

e. Grounding and Shielding: Ensure proper grounding of the LED controller, power supplies, and pixel LED system to minimise signal interference. Consider using shielded cables to reduce electromagnetic interference (EMI) and improve signal quality.

f. Check and Update Firmware: Verify that the LED controller's firmware is up to date. Manufacturers often release firmware updates to address software-related issues and improve data transmission performance. Follow the manufacturer's instructions for updating the firmware.

g. Test and Verify: After implementing power injection and data signal correction techniques, test the pixel LED system to ensure that the power distribution is stable and the data signals are accurately received by the pixels. Verify that colour output, brightness, and synchronisation are consistent across the system.

It is important to follow the manufacturer's guidelines, specifications, and best practices when performing power injection and data signal correction in a pixel LED system. If you are unsure or inexperienced, consult with a qualified technician or seek assistance from an authorised service centre specialising in pixel LED systems.

5.5 Testing the Repaired Pixel LED System

After performing repairs and addressing issues in a pixel LED system, it is essential to thoroughly test the system to ensure that the repairs were successful and that the system is functioning optimally. In this section, we will discuss the steps involved in testing the repaired pixel LED system.

1. Power Supply Verification: a. Check the power supply connections to ensure that they are securely connected and provide the correct voltage and current to the pixel LED system. b. Measure the voltage at various points in the system to verify that it falls within the specified range. c. Use a multimeter or a power supply tester to check for any fluctuations or irregularities in the power supply.
2. Visual Inspection: a. Visually inspect the entire pixel LED system for any visible issues, such as loose connections,

damaged cables, or misaligned pixels. b. Ensure that all components, including the LED controller, pixels, and connectors, are securely in place and properly connected.

3. Functional Testing: a. Turn on the pixel LED system and check if all pixels are functioning correctly. b. Verify that each pixel displays the expected colours, brightness levels, and patterns. c. Run different test sequences or pre-programmed lighting effects to assess the overall functionality of the system. d. Pay attention to any areas that previously experienced issues and ensure they are now functioning properly.

4. Colour Consistency and Calibration: a. Evaluate the colour consistency across the entire pixel LED system. Ensure that neighbouring pixels or sections display consistent colours and brightness levels. b. Adjust colour calibration settings on the LED controller, if applicable, to achieve accurate and uniform colour output.

5. Signal Testing: a. Test the data transmission and reception between the LED controller and the pixels. b. Verify that all pixels respond correctly to the control signals and synchronise properly. c. Test the system's response to changes in colour, brightness, or animation commands from the LED controller.

6. Performance and Stress Testing: a. Push the system to its limits by running intensive or complex lighting effects, colour transitions, and animations. b. Observe the system's performance and ensure that it can handle the load without issues such as flickering, lag, or unresponsive pixels.

7. Documentation: a. Maintain detailed documentation of the testing process, including any observed issues, their resolutions, and the overall performance of the repaired pixel LED system. b. This documentation will serve as a reference for future maintenance and troubleshooting.

If any issues are identified during testing, repeat the necessary repair steps or consult the manufacturer's technical support or a qualified technician for further assistance. Regularly inspect and test the pixel LED system to ensure ongoing functionality and performance.

Chapter 6: Preventive Maintenance and Tips

6.1 Importance of Regular Maintenance

Regular maintenance is essential for the longevity and optimal performance of PAR lights, SMPS, and pixel LED systems. It helps prevent potential issues, extends the lifespan of the equipment, and ensures that they operate reliably. In this chapter, we will discuss the importance of regular maintenance for these systems.

1. Equipment Longevity: Regular maintenance helps prolong the lifespan of PAR lights, SMPS, and pixel LED systems. By identifying and addressing minor issues early on, you can prevent them from escalating into major problems that may require costly repairs or replacement of components.

2. Performance Optimization: Proper maintenance ensures that the equipment operates at its best. Regular cleaning, calibration, and inspection help maintain optimal performance, colour accuracy, and brightness levels. This is crucial for PAR lights to deliver the desired lighting effects, SMPS to provide stable power supply, and pixel LED systems to display vibrant and synchronised visuals.

3. Enhanced Reliability: Regular maintenance minimises the risk of unexpected failures or malfunctions during important events or performances. By regularly checking and servicing the equipment, you can detect and resolve potential issues, ensuring that they function reliably when needed.

4. Cost Savings: Preventive maintenance can save you money in the long run. By proactively addressing issues and performing routine maintenance, you can avoid costly emergency repairs or replacements. It is generally more cost-effective to invest in regular maintenance than to deal with the consequences of neglected equipment.

5. Safety Assurance: Maintenance also plays a crucial role in

ensuring the safety of PAR lights, SMPS, and pixel LED systems. Regular inspections can identify potential electrical or mechanical hazards, such as frayed cables or loose connections, that could pose a safety risk. By promptly addressing these issues, you can maintain a safe working environment.

6. Compliance with Warranty and Insurance: Regular maintenance may be a requirement for maintaining warranty coverage or complying with insurance policies. It is important to check the terms and conditions of your warranty or insurance agreements to understand any maintenance obligations.

7. Documentation and Record-Keeping: Keep detailed records of all maintenance activities, including inspections, repairs, and replacements. This documentation serves as a reference for future maintenance, troubleshooting, and warranty claims. It helps track the history of the equipment, ensures consistency in maintenance practices, and provides valuable insights into the performance and reliability of the systems.

Remember, each type of equipment may have specific maintenance requirements outlined by the manufacturer. Follow their guidelines and recommendations for maintenance intervals, cleaning procedures, and any specific considerations for your PAR lights, SMPS, and pixel LED systems. Regular maintenance will help keep your equipment in optimal condition and ensure their longevity and reliable performance.

6.2 Cleaning and Care for Longevity

Proper cleaning and care are essential for maintaining the longevity and optimal performance of PAR lights, SMPS, and pixel LED systems. Regular cleaning helps prevent dust buildup, keeps the equipment in good condition, and ensures reliable operation. In this section, we will discuss cleaning and care tips for these systems.

1. Cleaning PAR Lights: a. Power Off: Before cleaning PAR lights, ensure that they are powered off and disconnected from the power source to avoid any electrical hazards.

    b. Dust Removal: Use a soft brush or compressed air to remove dust and debris from the outer surface of the PAR lights. Pay attention to the ventilation areas and cooling fans, as dust accumulation can affect their performance.

    c. Lens Cleaning: Clean the lenses of the PAR lights using a lens cleaning solution and a lint-free cloth. Gently wipe the lenses in a circular motion to remove smudges or fingerprints. Avoid using abrasive materials that may scratch the lens surface.

    d. Reflectors and Internal Cleaning: If necessary, remove the PAR light's casing to access the reflectors and internal components. Use compressed air or a soft brush to clean the reflectors and other internal areas. Be cautious not to touch or damage any electrical connections.

    e. Cable Inspection: Check the power cables and signal cables for any signs of wear or damage. Replace any frayed or damaged cables to ensure safe and reliable operation.

2. Cleaning SMPS: a. Power Off: Before cleaning SMPS, ensure that it is powered off and disconnected from the power source to prevent electrical accidents.

    b. Exterior Cleaning: Use a soft, dry cloth to clean the external surface of the SMPS. Remove any dust or dirt buildup to prevent interference with the cooling system.

c. Ventilation Cleaning: Clear any dust or debris from the ventilation openings and cooling fans using compressed air or a soft brush. This helps maintain proper airflow and prevents overheating.

d. Internal Cleaning: If necessary, carefully open the SMPS casing to access the internal components. Use compressed air or a soft brush to remove dust from the circuit boards and other internal areas. Take caution not to touch or damage any sensitive components.

e. Cable Inspection: Inspect the power cables and connectors for any damage or signs of wear. Replace any faulty or damaged cables to ensure safe and reliable operation.

3. Cleaning Pixel LED Systems: a. Power Off: Turn off the pixel LED system and disconnect it from the power source before cleaning to prevent electrical hazards.

   b. Exterior Cleaning: Use a soft, dry cloth to clean the external surfaces of the pixel LED system, including the LED controller, pixel panels, and connectors. Remove any dust or dirt that may have accumulated.

   c. Pixel Panel Cleaning: Follow the manufacturer's guidelines for cleaning the pixel panels. Depending on the type of panels, use a microfiber cloth or a mild cleaning solution recommended by the manufacturer. Avoid applying excessive pressure or using abrasive materials that may damage the panels.

   d. Cable Inspection: Inspect the cables and connectors for any damage, loose connections, or signs of wear. Replace any faulty cables or connectors to maintain reliable operation.

4. General Cleaning Tips: a. Avoid Liquids: Do not use liquid cleaners directly on the equipment. Instead, apply the cleaner to a soft cloth or sponge and then gently clean the surfaces.

b. Avoid Abrasives: Avoid using abrasive materials, harsh chemicals, or abrasive cleaners that can scratch or damage the equipment.

c. Regular Maintenance: Perform cleaning regularly to prevent the buildup of dust, dirt, or grime, which can affect the performance.

6.3 Best Practices for Extending the Lifespan of Components

To ensure the longevity and reliable performance of PAR lights, SMPS, and pixel LED systems, it is important to follow best practices for component care and maintenance. By implementing these practices, you can extend the lifespan of the equipment and minimise the risk of failures or malfunctions. In this section, we will discuss some best practices to consider.

1. Proper Power Management: a. Use Reliable Power Sources: Ensure that the PAR lights, SMPS, and pixel LED systems are connected to stable and properly grounded power sources to prevent power fluctuations or surges that can damage the components.

   b. Avoid Overloading: Do not overload the power supply with excessive equipment or draw more power than the capacity of the system. Check the power requirements of the equipment and ensure that the power supply is adequate.

   c. Use Surge Protectors: Install surge protectors or voltage stabilisers to safeguard the equipment against power spikes or electrical surges.

2. Adequate Ventilation: a. Maintain Proper Airflow: Ensure that the PAR lights, SMPS, and pixel LED systems have adequate ventilation to dissipate heat effectively. Avoid placing them in enclosed spaces or blocking ventilation openings.

   b. Clean Cooling Components: Regularly clean the cooling fans and vents to remove dust and debris that can obstruct airflow and cause overheating.

3. Safe Handling and Transportation: a. Handle with Care: When moving or handling PAR lights, SMPS, and pixel LED systems, exercise caution to avoid dropping or jarring the components, which can lead to internal damage.

   b. Secure Transportation: During transportation, use

appropriate packaging or cases to protect the equipment from physical impact or vibration.

4. Avoid Excessive Heat and Humidity: a. Avoid Extreme Temperatures: Keep the PAR lights, SMPS, and pixel LED systems away from extreme heat sources, direct sunlight, or extremely cold environments, as these conditions can affect the performance and lifespan of the components.
b. Control Humidity Levels: High humidity can cause moisture-related issues in electronic components. Maintain a suitable humidity level in the storage and operating environment.

5. Regular Inspections: a. Visual Inspections: Conduct visual inspections of the PAR lights, SMPS, and pixel LED systems to identify any visible signs of damage, loose connections, or wear. Address any issues promptly.
b. Component Checks: Regularly check the cables, connectors, circuit boards, and other internal components for signs of wear, damage, or corrosion. Replace any faulty components as needed.

6. Follow Manufacturer Guidelines: a. Refer to the Manufacturer's Documentation: Follow the manufacturer's guidelines for installation, usage, maintenance, and troubleshooting of the PAR lights, SMPS, and pixel LED systems. These guidelines are specific to the equipment and can help ensure optimal performance and longevity.
b. Firmware and Software Updates: Stay updated with the latest firmware or software releases provided by the manufacturer. These updates may include bug fixes, performance improvements, or new features that enhance the equipment's functionality.

7. Regular Calibration and Testing: a. Calibrate Color and Brightness: Periodically calibrate the colour accuracy and

brightness levels of the PAR lights and pixel LED systems using calibration tools or software provided by the manufacturer.
b. Conduct Performance Tests: Perform regular performance tests to verify the functionality and synchronisation of the pixel LED systems, ensuring that all pixels respond correctly to control signals.

By following these best practices, you can maximise the lifespan and reliability of PAR lights, SMPS, and pixel LED systems. Regular maintenance, safe handling, and adherence to manufacturer guidelines are key to ensuring optimal performance.

6.4 Software Updates and Firmware Upgrades of Pixel LED Systems
Software updates and firmware upgrades play a crucial role in maintaining the optimal performance and functionality of pixel LED systems. Manufacturers often release updates to address bugs, introduce new features, enhance performance, or improve compatibility. In this section, we will discuss the importance of software updates and firmware upgrades for pixel LED systems and how to perform them effectively.

1. Benefits of Software Updates and Firmware Upgrades: a. Bug Fixes: Updates often include fixes for known bugs or issues reported by users. Applying these updates can help resolve any glitches or unexpected behaviour in the pixel LED system.
    b. Performance Enhancements: Manufacturers may release updates to optimise the performance of the pixel LED system, improving colour accuracy, refresh rates, or overall responsiveness.
    c. New Features: Updates may introduce new features or functionalities that enhance the capabilities of the pixel LED system. These additions can expand the creative possibilities and allow for more dynamic visual displays.
    d. Compatibility Improvements: Updates may address compatibility issues with external devices, control protocols, or software systems, ensuring seamless integration and operation.
2. Preparing for Software Updates and Firmware Upgrades: a. Backup Data: Before performing any updates, it is essential to back up your existing settings, configurations, and content on the pixel LED system. This ensures that you can restore your previous setup in case of any unexpected issues during the update process.
    b. Read Documentation: Review the manufacturer's documentation, release notes, or user manuals accompanying the update to understand the changes, installation

requirements, and any specific instructions provided.

c. Verify System Compatibility: Check if your pixel LED system is compatible with the software update or firmware upgrade. Some updates may only be applicable to specific models or hardware versions.

3. Performing Software Updates and Firmware Upgrades: a. Obtain the Update: Visit the manufacturer's website or official support channels to download the latest software update or firmware upgrade specific to your pixel LED system.

    b. Installation Steps: Follow the provided instructions carefully for installing the update. This may involve transferring the update file to the pixel LED system via USB, SD card, or using specialised software tools provided by the manufacturer.

    c. Power and Connectivity: Ensure a stable power source and a reliable network connection (if applicable) during the update process. Power interruptions or unstable connections can disrupt the update and potentially cause issues.

    d. Follow Progress Indicators: During the update, follow any progress indicators or on-screen instructions provided by the pixel LED system. Avoid interrupting or disconnecting the system until the update process is complete.

4. Post-Update Testing and Calibration: a. Verify Functionality: After the update is complete, thoroughly test the pixel LED system to ensure all features, controls, and functionalities are working as expected.

    b. Content Validation: Verify that any pre-existing content or configurations are intact and functioning correctly after the update. Make any necessary adjustments or reapply settings if needed.

    c. Calibration and Fine-Tuning: If the update includes changes to colour calibration, refresh rates, or other visual parameters, consider performing calibration or fine-tuning procedures to optimise the display quality.

By regularly updating the software and firmware of your pixel LED system, you can enjoy improved performance, new features, and bug fixes. Keeping your system up to date ensures a smoother operation, enhances compatibility, and allows you to take full advantage of the capabilities of your pixel LED system.

Conclusion

Congratulations! You have completed the "DIY Guide to Repairing PAR Lights, 12V SMPS, 5V SMPS, and Pixel LED Systems." With the knowledge and skills gained from this eBook, you are now well-prepared to troubleshoot and repair various lighting systems. Remember to adhere to safety guidelines and continue exploring new techniques and advancements in the lighting industry. Happy repairing!

Disclaimer

This Book is intended for educational and informational purposes only. Always exercise caution when dealing with electrical systems and seek professional assistance if unsure about any repair procedures. The author and publisher disclaim any liability for damages resulting from the use of the information provided in this Book.